The Consequences of Love

The Consequences of Love

Finding Family, Faith, and Freedom Through an Unexpected Gift

Dianna Finewood

ABUNDANT HARVEST
PUBLISHING

Editing/Formatting: Erik V. Sahakian
Cover Design/Layout: Andrew Enos

All Scripture is taken from the New King James Version of the
Bible. Copyright © 1979, 1980, 1982 by Thomas Nelson, Inc.
Used by permission. All rights reserved.

Library of Congress Control Number: 2021916012

ISBN 978-1-7349949-9-5
First Printing: October 2021

FOR INFORMATION CONTACT:

Abundant Harvest Publishing
35145 Oak Glen Rd
Yucaipa, CA 92399
www.abundantharvestpublishing.com

Printed in the United States of America

For all those who have felt lost, felt alone, felt overwhelmed—there is hope in love.

Come meet Him...

Contents

*"Yes, I have loved you with an everlasting love;
therefore with lovingkindness I have drawn you."*

~ Jeremiah 31:3

Chapter 1

The excitement was palpable. This was our second visit. We had already heard the baby's heartbeat at the first appointment. This visit was simply to confirm things were progressing along safely...and to share this joy with our 14-year-old daughter who was patiently seated in the waiting room. We had just made it past the vulnerable 12-week mark and we wanted our daughter to see her future brother or sister.

The ultrasound process had begun when we noticed my doctor's facial expression change from joy to concern.

"I'm having a hard time finding the heartbeat," she said. "Let me go get a colleague for help." She quietly exited the room.

I couldn't look at my husband. I couldn't breathe. The lump in my throat made it impossible to swallow. The crushing sensation in my chest surpassed the burning in my eyes as they filled, uncontrollably, with tears. This cannot be happening...again.

My medical chart summarized my visit succinctly: Miscarriage # 3. However, my heart didn't share this simple summary. Why did we lose another baby?

***

I find it fascinating when adults can recall vivid details of their childhood. Particularly, early childhood memories. I can't do that. My memories are more like short video clips with kindergarten being the earliest memory I can recollect.

What I *do* remember is the most beautiful woman in my life. She was perfect. She was always by my side and she was in every one of my earliest, most precious memories. No, she's not my mother. She's my sister.

Jennifer is only four years older than me, but in my eyes, she was a graceful queen! I wanted to be just like her. I'd sneak into her makeup bag, trying to perfect the art of eyeshadow and mascara. I did my best to imitate her look. I'd dress up in her clothes when she wasn't around. I even started shaving my legs in an effort to copy her...I was only in first grade! She had beauty. She had style. She had fun friends. But, sadly, she had a dark side.

By the time she was 12 years old she was addicted to drugs. Her pain needed numbing. Drugs will do that, but they don't just take away the pain, they take away everything. The destruction and rippling of consequences can take decades to mend.

But I'm getting ahead of myself.

Jennifer and I lived with our grandparents. They were amazing people. My grandpa was a hero and one of the finest men I know. I believe I was the apple of his eye! My grandma, whose thick Russian accent made some words too hard to understand, was a kind and loving lady who labored endlessly over my sister and me. Together, they showered us with love, kindness, and affection. Truly, my heart is filled with happy memories of them.

For the early 80s, we weren't your typical family: two elderly grandparents caring for two confused children, but we sure did make fine memories! Some of my best were eating dinner together. Whether dipping my french fries in my chocolate shake at Bob's Big Boy (those who know me now and what a healthy eater I am are probably laughing aloud), to staying home and eating Kentucky Fried

Chicken at our dinner table. Those mashed potatoes were magical!

Saturday morning memories were of watching *Scooby-Doo* and being adorned in pj's. I loved snuggling with my sister. My grandma loved making us breakfast while we lay in front of the TV. Dunkin' eggs were my favorite on Grandma's menu. I was privileged to coin them with such a unique name. Truthfully, my reasoning was simple: I'd dunk the toast in the eggs, so they must be called, "dunkin' eggs"! I thought simply back then.

Our tiny living room was open to the kitchen in my grandparents' house. It was a small home, but it was clean and I remember feeling wanted. It was perched on a busy street in Covina. My grandpa, who made an extremely modest living, repaired lawnmowers from our garage.

I absolutely loved this because it allowed me to be with my grandpa even while he was working. I was always tinkering around with his tools or playing on his lawnmower lift as if it were an elevator. I was a dedicated elevator lift attendant, in my humble opinion.

When I was six or seven years old I added to my

repertoire of job skills. I would pretend to "drive to work." My grandpa would actually let me sit in his old white Dodge pick-up truck that was parked in our driveway. One day I must have really been serious about my commute because I unintentionally knocked the column shifter from park to neutral. Our driveway was on a slight hill. Did I mention we lived on a busy street?

I began to panic as the truck rolled back. My grandpa, who walked with a cane, was in no way capable of running after the truck and stopping it. I didn't know what to do!

Fortunately, my grandpa's grandson, George Jr., happened to be visiting that day. He and his wife were always really nice to me. I remember they were very much into yoga and one day helped me get into a lotus pose. They were so impressed that I could actually do it that I refused to get out of it. I wanted to make them proud. So, I sat and stayed in that pose for so long that I could no longer feel my feet! Eventually, I called for their help and they came to untangle my legs!

It turned out I needed their help again the day I "drove" my grandpa's truck into traffic.

Fortunately, George Jr. ran to the rescue...literally! He immediately raced out into the street, waving the cars to stop. He managed to stop the truck and then asked me to climb aside while he drove it back into the driveway. I thought my grandpa would kill me. I was shaking with fear from the incident and from what my grandpa would do to me.

The funny thing is I never even remember my grandpa yelling at me. The only thing I remember are chocks being faithfully placed behind the truck tires from that day forward. This speaks of the gentle and loving spirit my grandpa showed me. That memory taught me so much.

My grandma was no different. Her great love to serve my sister and me is almost incomprehensible! She tirelessly prepared breakfast, lunch, and dinner...day after day. I never once heard her complain.

She would greet us every morning and help me pick out my clothes. Because their income was limited, I remember my grandma making me clothes. She was a beautiful seamstress. She made stunning dresses professionally. She even taught me how to sew. I made some pretty fancy Barbie dresses in my day!

At lunchtime my grandpa would mosey in from the garage and enjoy my grandma's homemade eats! During the summer, when I wasn't in school, I would often join him and we'd watch an episode of *The Munsters*. It was a marvelous time and some of my favorite memories.

During the school year, my grandpa would faithfully drive me to school each morning and be waiting for me in the afternoon. Most days, there was a trip to Thrifty's for a triple scoop of ice cream. I remember him asking me one day if I wanted to invite a friend for our ice cream trip, but the time spent with my grandpa was so precious to me that I didn't want to share him with anyone. I remember feeling bad, kinda selfish. Now, looking back, it warms my heart knowing how deeply I loved him and longed for time spent with him...especially since those years would be short-lived.

With such loving grandparents and a peaceful home, you may be wondering why, at the age of 12, my sister needed numbing? Our childhood seemed so special. And, with my grandparents, it was. But remember I mentioned my earliest memories only go back to kindergarten? I don't even remember why we were living with my grandparents.

I don't even remember having a relationship with my mother. Sure, I knew I *had* a mother. I just can't recall her or have memories of her in those earliest years of my life.

The memories I do have of my mother came a little later. I remember my sister and I would go visit her for the weekend. They were fun for me. After all, my mom would have exotic boyfriends who would share their unusual fare with us and broaden my taste buds. I learned Pakistani food is absolutely amazing!

When my mom was done with the exotic boyfriends, she married an American man. No fancy cuisine but I really liked him. He was funny and he would make my mom laugh. Her new husband was always nice to me and I would look forward to our visits.

Over time, though, fights between my mother and her husband began to brew. Then they became more explosive and physically violent. I remember during one weekend visit I wanted to go back to my grandparents. I never mentioned it though because I was afraid to speak up.

Eventually, their fights became more and more normal. Soon I was accustomed to their pattern. They would fight. They would make up. Repeat.

Despite the fighting, which only appeared visible behind closed doors, there were plenty of good times between my mom, her husband, my sister, and me. I was getting used to their "pattern" when I'd visit. Also, the make-up times were a lot of fun and we made fantastic memories! One of which was taking a trip to the historic Olvera Street in downtown Los Angeles. They lived in Echo Park so when I would visit we'd often enjoy the highlights of Los Angeles. My sister was always by my side, so I felt complete!

To others, my mom appeared stable enough in this marriage that eventually she requested my sister and I come live with her. To be honest, I was excited for this new move. I thought it would be an adventure.

I felt that my sister and I were genuinely welcomed into their home. Or, at least that's the video clip I have in my seven-year-old mind. However, one night in particular solidified the need to change how I felt about this new living arrangement. It became gruesomely evident that my mom's fights with her husband had escalated. Brutally escalated. My mom's husband was no longer satisfied releasing his fury on her. Now it was my sister's turn. My beautiful sister.

I don't recall how it started—the beginning or the end. I just remember the fight. I don't recollect my mother even in the room once the beating began on my sister. What I do recall is...I was. I was in that room witnessing a rage that to this day still makes my eyes well with tears. How could anyone beat another human being with such fury and madness? Nothing stopped him. Not her screams. Not her tears. Not her blood. I just sat there crying, hiding under the kitchen table, watching in horror as his violent punches poured more and more blood from my 12-year-old sister's body.

I wanted so badly to get up from under the table and scream at him, "STOP! You're going to kill her! STOP!" But I couldn't speak. Fear had crippled me. I felt like I had no voice. Even worse, I kept silent (a guilt that still plagues me to this day) because if he stopped assaulting her, he might come after me.

My next memory of that night was of my sister

and me boarding a bus. It was the middle of the night. My sister and I were running away. I don't remember all the details. I remember it was cool but not cold. It was dark and it was quiet. I remember the bus we got on. However, I didn't know where we were going or how we even paid the bus fee. We even hitchhiked part of the way, but I don't remember much of those details either. All I knew was I wanted to be with my sister and I wanted to be far from that place. Far away from that fear.

The bus rides and hitchhikes landed us at my grandparents in Covina, CA. It was still dark. Early morning. When my grandparents saw the blows my sister's body had taken it was evident the police needed to be called. Also, my father and stepmother were called.

The police arrived, took their reports, and gave me two options. I could return to my mother's apartment or I could go home with my father and stepmother. Well, that was a no brainer! Of course my sister and I would go with my dad and stepmom. Sadly, it was explained to me this was not an option. Since my sister and I had different fathers, and hers was unknown, she couldn't go with me to my father's. She was allowed to stay living with my grandparents, but I could not. I had a father and stepmother who were willing to let me live with them.

My dad even told me that if I chose to live with them he would buy me a puppy so I wouldn't be lonely. A puppy? My seven-year-old self-chose to live with my father and *not* my mother.

Chapter 2

The first night in my dad's home felt...sterile. I had my own room. I had a stepsister. I had a stepbrother. I had a stepmom. Soon I would have a puppy! Yet, inside I felt incredibly lonely, isolated, and immeasurably sad. I missed my "Jennifer" and I missed the kindness and warmth of my grandparents.

An unfamiliar comfort, for the first time, came to me late one night. I was lying on my side, in bed, staring at my nightlight. I don't recall when or how I acquired this picture, but there above my nightlight was a picture of Jesus knocking on a brown wood door. He was dressed in white. There was a golden glow around Him. His expression was kind. It was loving. It drew me in and when I looked at it I felt safe. I felt less lonely. Many nights I would fall asleep just staring at that picture. I don't recall ever going to church and I had never even seen a Bible. My dad and stepmom certainly didn't go to church, either. So how this picture came to live over my nightlight I will never know! All I knew was that it brought me something special. It really was a peace that surpassed understanding.

I wish I could say from that point forward I gave my heart to Jesus and walked with Him closely. But, that's not my story. Not at that point anyway.

My whole world, as I knew it, was completely different. I went from having homemade breakfast made by my grandma to making cereal for myself. My stepmom and dad left early in the mornings for work and were gone before I even got up. My older sister and brother were home, but they were busy getting their own selves ready. And, they were teenagers...they were on an entirely different, much cooler level than me. I was just doing my best trying to find out where I fit in with this new family.

I would ride my bike to my new school which was a journey in and of itself because I was not accustomed, at second grade, to crossing busy streets. Let's just say I learned to be aware of my surroundings really quick! Fortunately, adjusting to school wasn't so bad. I did my best to fit in and I made friends easily.

I was starting to find my place and fit in at home, too. I was adjusting despite not having my grandparents or Jennifer with me. I missed them deeply though. It wasn't the same sleeping without Jennifer. We had always shared a bed and it felt lonely without her, but I had my picture of Jesus! My dad and stepmom kept their word about a puppy, too! They sincerely enjoyed surprising us kids. One night, they did just that!

I was already in bed, nearly asleep, when my dad called for me. Actually, he yelled for me. I distinctly remember thinking I might be in trouble. I hopped out of bed and walked down the hall questioning myself, *Did I forget to take out the trash?* I was afraid and anticipated the worst! But, I wasn't in trouble. In fact, I went from fear to indescribable joy in just seconds as my eyes discovered the blonde ball of fur sleeping in my stepmom's arms. A puppy! *My* puppy! I was shaking with anticipation to scoop that precious pet in my arms. Her sweet breath and sleepy brown eyes had my heart hooked instantly.

I named her Ginger and she quickly became the best friend I needed. I was too young then to realize how therapeutic she really was to me. Back then, she just made me happy! And, she started my lifelong love for animals!

If that wasn't great enough, it kept getting better! My stepmom had a love for horses and would take us kids to the stables where she kept them. I longed for my very own horse. They are such beautiful creatures. So majestic. So gentle, yet powerful. A favorite quote of mine is by Winston Churchill that reads:

"There is something about the outside of a horse that is good for the inside of a man."

After it became apparent that I truly loved horses, my dad and stepmom sought to find me a pony. I still remember the day my pony arrived at the ranch. I was riding with my cousin when we saw a truck and trailer pull up. We watched and wondered who got a new horse. Then my beautiful pony stepped off the trailer. I didn't know what to do! My cousin shouted, "Go get your pony!" I ran so fast I nearly fell as my scrawny legs dashed at top speed. She was a beautiful bay pony with a thick black mane and tail. All four black socks. And the kindest eyes graced the sweetest face I'd ever seen. I'd heard stories that ponies, especially mares, can be feisty. Not my sweet girl! We bonded instantly and it was as if she knew exactly what I needed. We became inseparable. I named her D.J. for Dianna Jane.

Whether we were taking professional riding lessons and attending shows, or just goofing off bareback and trying to learn equestrian vaulting, she would do it all! The trail rides we would go on were also some of the greatest memories! Countless hours were spent with her!

Unfortunately, despite the precious animals in my life, my teenage years were rough for me. I think for most kids the teenage years are rough. The traumatic events from my childhood were starting to have an effect on me. My dad and stepmom were never physically abusive, but they sure could fight! They would scream so loudly at each other and the vocal rage my dad unleashed left me wanting to hide and be anyplace but in the middle of the storm. I was so scared that at any moment blood would be shed like I witnessed as a small child. Fortunately, the fights never reached that degree. Nonetheless, they always left me shaken.

Also, no one ever said, "I love you." Looking back, that's so sad. I remember the first time my father said he loved me was when I was almost 20 years old...and that was *after* I said it first. I don't fault him; he's not an affectionate man, but the lack of knowing I was loved and wanted really began to disturb my mind.

I remember wanting to withdraw more and more. I was already an introvert, but it became even worse. I started suffering from anxiety and depression. Every time my parents came home from work, I was sure I would be in trouble for a chore I forgot to do. My heart would race as they pulled up the driveway. I would feel an overwhelming sense of panic.

By the time I was in 8th grade I had already attempted suicide. This landed me in a mental hospital which, unfortunately, did nothing to help the depressive thoughts I battled. It also took a toll on my father and stepmom and I could feel the tension between them. I didn't want them to suffer, too.

Even worse, feeling unloved and unwanted was becoming a core thread inside of me and a mental battle I had no weapons to fight. Even the therapy I received in the hospital left me ill-equipped to handle the depression and fearful thoughts that ran rampant in my mind.

By the time I was 17 years old, I had put myself

in such compromising situations and places that it left me being raped on three different occasions. First by a teenage boy. Second by a teacher. And last by an older man. These attacks left me feeling like a dirty rag that needed to be discarded. Like garbage. I had no value for myself and I had no idea what a healthy and loving relationship should be like. Tragically with this mindset, I willingly continued to see the older man who initially attacked me.

My warped way of thinking lured me toward a false hope that if a sincere relationship formed between us, then it would justify the attack, and that he actually loved me and didn't want to hurt me. I even dreamed of marrying him and would visit him whenever I could. This inappropriate and despicable relationship continued for several years. He would sexually abuse my body, but he would also tell me how pretty I was and hold me and cuddle me afterward. I felt so disgusted from the sex, but I longed to receive his hugs and affection so badly! I remember him even kissing the top of my head while hugging me. I longed to feel loved and I thought this must be what it's like. So, I learned to disconnect from my physical body because I detested having vulgar sex with him and instead focused on the cuddling that would happen afterward. I would cry when he cuddled me.

To say that I was mentally scarred would be an understatement. I was convinced that if he would just marry me it would make all the pain worth it.

However, it was during this same time that something much better came into my life. I went to a Bible study with a friend and, after hearing about God and His great and faithful love for us, I accepted Jesus Christ as my Lord and savior. I recalled the picture I had of Jesus when I was only seven years old. All those years He was longing to have a relationship with me. To show me true love and a better way to live. His desire was to heal me and fill my heart with His love. A pure love. A love that never fails.

So, at first, I stopped seeing this older man and I went to church. This was a big deal because *no one* in my family went to church! I got teased by my dad each time I went. My dad meant no ill will when he would lightheartedly mock me about attending church. He had no idea of the mess I had gotten myself into. When I heard those words of hope, love, and joy it fed my starving soul. I wanted this kind of faith! My heart *needed* this kind of love!

Sadly, though, teenage "life" and stressors that accompany it robbed me of my Christian mindset. I remember getting into a fight with my parents and going to visit the older man again. I was so upset from the fight that I wanted to hurt myself. I knew rekindling the relationship would hurt me. So I went. And because of the guilt and shame, I stopped going to church and reading my Bible.

Honestly, in retrospect, it overwhelms my heart that Jesus was reaching out to me the entire time I was seeing this older man. I see now the parallel of two "loves." An imposter of what *I* thought was love, versus the truth or what *Jesus* longed to show me as love. He was there all along. Always waiting. Never giving up on me. However, at that time in my life, I chose to give up on Him...or at least walk away from Him.

When I was 18 I wanted nothing more than to move out of my parents' home. I began dating another older man, but since he was only seven years older than me, and a good family friend, my parents approved of this relationship. Before long, I moved in with him.

I was in no mental condition to be in a healthy relationship, nor did I even know what one looked like. So, I floundered in this relationship but stayed for over three years. I think we both knew it wasn't right. I had healing to do and was incapable of giving or receiving love. I just didn't know how long it would take to sort out the pain and damage. So, at 21, I moved out and rented a room from a friend. I enrolled in a local community college. I worked full-time during the day and took classes at night. I wasn't yet sure of my path, but this seemed the most productive way to better myself. I also didn't want to date *anyone!*

Chapter 3

Like a typical 22-year-old who *isn't* walking with Jesus, I justified that my intense week of work and college studies needed rewarding. So, I filled my weekends with nightclubs and partying. I was still adamant about avoiding dating, but I wanted to dance and have fun.

That "staying single" mindset lasted about six months.

The first time I laid eyes on the love of my life was a night to remember. I was with a group of friends at a local bar eagerly awaiting an opportunity to line dance.

I happened to walk by a friend from high school, said hello to her, and continued on to the ladies' restroom. Unbeknownst to me, my future husband, who was her roommate at the time, asked how she knew me. He requested an introduction.

So, later that evening, she approached me. She pitched that there was this great guy I just *had* to meet. I was reluctant. Meeting a man...in a bar? Aren't there endless warnings about this kind of encounter? This was the antithesis of what I wanted! No more relationships! However, I found myself agreeing to meet him and followed her.

We crossed to the other side of the bar. She tapped his shoulder. He was conversing with several other guys. I had low expectations. When he turned around, however, and our eyes suddenly met, I was delighted that I had agreed to this encounter. To say he was easy on the eyes doesn't do him justice. His chiseled jaw, warm smile, and speckled goldish-brown eyes had me captivated. A well-groomed goatee framed his full lips. He was the most handsome man under a cowboy hat that I'd ever seen.

My friend walked off to allow this cute cowboy and me to talk. He reached out his hand, introduced himself as David, then politely excused himself so he could finish his previous conversation with his buddies. He turned right around and left me standing alone, staring at his back. Yep, this really happened.

Most ladies would have turned on their heels and marched right off if a man did this. I stood there, feeling awkward, but I stood there. About five seconds passed (the awkwardness made it feel like five minutes!). When he turned back around he gave me his full attention. That night he made me feel like I was the only girl in that place. Even though there was a sea of beautiful women around us, his eyes were fixed on me. The entire time.

It would be great to say our relationship was magical and perfect from the very start, but that would be an utter lie. David had no idea of the "adventure" he was about to embark on with me.

While my teenage years were tumultuous, Jennifer's were none the better. In fact, they were far worse. The dark lifestyle of drugs and all sorts of illegal activity to numb her pain had gripped her. She was only fifteen when she gave birth to my nephew. The physical violence that she experienced as a child repeated itself. Her relationships were wickedly abusive.

When it became evident that she was in no way capable of caring for her son, she had him move in with friends. This only seemed to cause my nephew even more damage, so I asked David what to do. We had only been dating four or five months, but David didn't hesitate. "Let's get an apartment and move him in with us," was his first response. Did I mention we had only been dating for a few months?

My sister and I, who once had been so close, had drifted apart. Sure, I would spend as much time with her as I could, but growing up in two different homes and being four years apart in age put a strain on us. She was forced to grow up fast. When I was about 13, I stayed the weekend with her and witnessed firsthand how she'd been living. My nephew was around two years old and they lived in an apartment with my nephew's father. My nephew's father was another violent man. It was all my sister knew. He beat her so badly one night that her entire bathroom was splattered with blood. The mirrors and shelves were broken, and my beautiful sister lay crumpled in the corner. The screams from my nephew when he saw her were unbearable. I grabbed him, ran out, and held him in my arms outside on the apartment stairs. I cried and told him it would be okay. It would be okay, but I didn't know *how* it would be okay.

This was the life my nephew first experienced and it only grew worse from there. Living in terrible neighborhoods exposed him to gang solicitation and more violence.

I remember visiting my sister when she lived in North Hollywood and witnessing a shooting one night. That was more than my heart could bear...and that was just one night. I can't even imagine what my nephew must have seen daily.

This was my nephew that David agreed to take in and help raise. We were clueless. I was damaged. My nephew was damaged. Yet, David's tenacity to never give up, coupled with a heart that hurt for what my family had been through, gave him strength to commit.

I would not be doing David's character justice if I didn't take time to commend this amazing man! He had his own share of difficulties. Losing his mom to breast cancer and watching his two younger brothers grow up without a mother was tragic. Not to mention the family divide that occurred over his mother's death. He had lost so much. Yet, he is a brave and stoic man. He has a way of fighting harder when the chips seem to be against him. So with the messy mental state of my nephew and me...let's just say the chips were definitely against him.

Chapter 4

Surprisingly, our instant-family situation was working. Well, most of the time. David was so loving to my nephew and me. We would go rollerblading around our apartment complex and play badminton in the front grass. We laughed a lot. We loved a lot. We were making wonderful memories.

David supported me so I could go to college full time. I put so much effort into my schooling that I achieved straight A's. I wanted to get into Loma Linda University and I knew nothing short of straight A's would make that happen.

Although my life was progressing positively, I still hadn't dealt with the baggage of my past relationships. Also, I wasn't giving my whole heart to David. I held back a lot. I started stupid quarrels. I was hoping he would end the relationship because, I think in a way, I didn't feel worthy of his love.

But David was a rock. He didn't give up. That's not his character. He continued to show me love, devotion, and encouragement.

Year after year he stood by me. He was the one to open up and read to me my Loma Linda University acceptance letter because I was too nervous to open it!

Even though I was still holding back from giving David my whole heart, our relationship, and my life in general, appeared to be moving in the right direction. My sister, however, was still struggling and couldn't seem to escape the lifestyle that numbed her pain.

My nephew's pain was becoming more evident, too. Trying to raise a teenage boy is a challenge in and of itself, but this sweet boy was broken. He longed for his mother. When she promised him a visit but failed to show, it devastated him. My sister, my nephew, and I were just so supremely damaged that we flat out fumbled while we walked through the rubble of our early lives.

***

When I was 25 years old, my sister told me she needed to talk to me. I met with her. She told me she was pregnant. I was shocked at first. My nephew was still living with me and I thought this news would devastate him. For her to have another child when he couldn't even live with her? I braced for the hurt he would feel, but Jennifer was so happy. Nervous, yes, but happy. She was even staying clean from drugs.

However, Jennifer's vision for her life to turn around was short-lived.

I never even met the man who got my sister pregnant. He was sentenced to life in prison shortly after she told me about the pregnancy. Jennifer was distraught. She had no place to live and her heart was shattered...again.

I was able to arrange a room for her to rent with the same friend that helped me when I needed a place to stay. Whenever possible, I would drive her to doctor's appointments for prenatal care.

It was during this time that something began stirring in me. I became more and more excited for this baby. I threw my sister a baby shower. I shopped for baby clothes. I found myself wanting to do things that had never been done in my family. Baby showers? My other sister and brother had babies when they were just teenagers, so I grew up listening to my father and stepmother lament at what a huge mistake they were making. I formulated in my brain that *children* were a huge mistake. I had never witnessed children being "celebrated" or even wanted! I even overheard my stepmom, after a fight, tell my father that she'd rather have another dog than me. Clearly I associated children with everything negative and nothing to be desired.

So, why then, was I drawn to this tiny baby growing inside my sister? I had never felt this kind of excitement...and *joy*.

The weeks turned into months and, after nine of them to be exact, the day finally arrived! Jennifer was in labor and we were headed to the hospital. She was far enough into labor that the hospital admitted her, but she still had hours to go. The staff suggested we walk. It seemed like hours that we walked the hospital floor. I did my best to crack jokes and make her laugh, hoping it would ease her pain. I could see her distress, but she was also incredibly tough. She actually made the whole process look easy! She wasn't given any pain medication. Being medically indigent didn't offer her any favors. So, she was going at this all natural, but her tenacity saw her through the birthing process.

David and I were honored to be by her side while my nephew sat just outside the birthing room. David stood quietly by her pillow, encouraging her that she could do this. He was so calm yet commanding. I was touched at how supportive he was for my sister.

I, on the other hand, wanted to see the birth process live! This was absolutely amazing and I couldn't wait to lay eyes on this precious little one. There was so much love and joy taking place. It was indescribable.

Then Maddison arrived. It was as if time stood still. I truthfully have never experienced something so beautiful. Something so innocent. Something so lovely. My heart overflowed with love and emotion as the doctor placed her in my arms. I was blessed to be the first to hold her. I couldn't stop staring at her tiny face. *She is absolutely perfect*, I thought.

From my arms she went to David's. Then to my nephew's. Then, finally, Maddison was placed in my sister's arms. Everything about that evening was beautiful and filled with love. An everlasting, special love and bond between us that words can never completely describe.

Chapter 5

Those first few months were blissful! My sister seemed so happy. However, as time continued on my sister began to relapse.

As much as I didn't want to see it, it was becoming evident my sister was slipping. Slipping back into the dark lifestyle she had been so familiar with.

It began slowly at first. We'd offer to watch Maddison for an evening and most of the time those "evenings" would turn into "weekends." David and I didn't mind though. We had a special bond with Maddison and we knew if she was with us she was safe and we could shower her with love. Before long, my nephew, David, and I found ourselves missing Maddison when she wasn't around!

***

Our first temporary guardianship was just that...temporary. I believed my sister would get back on her feet as she promised she would.

However, our second guardianship, a year and a half later, left me doubting. My sister called us from jail. We rushed to get Maddison.

It was during this second guardianship that David and I even consulted a family law attorney over our concern for Maddison and the lifestyle she would be exposed to should she go back with my sister. We pleaded with the attorney that it would only be a matter of time before Maddison would be exposed to physical, sexual, or emotional abuse if she returned to the environment my sister was living in. Still, the attorney turned us away and told us it's next to impossible to terminate maternal rights in the state of California.

When my sister was released from jail she came for Maddison. We were devastated.

My life was a dichotomy. I was about to graduate from the dental hygiene program at Loma Linda University and, despite all I had put David through, he'd proposed to me! We were planning our marriage and honeymoon while, at the same time, I was prepping for my dental hygiene boards. My heart was filled with excitement, but, my nephew, after five years of living with us, decided he wanted to move in with Jennifer and Maddison. Since he was 17 years old, and we only had temporary guardianship of him, he could make that decision.

I genuinely understood why he wanted to live with my sister. He loved her deeply and she was all he longed for. Plus, Maddison was there, too. So, while my "head" understood his decision, my heart was broken.

There were days when I would succumb to the sadness of losing my nephew and Maddison, but then the joy of my upcoming marriage, honeymoon, and the adventure of a new career on the horizon would lift my spirit. And, fortunately, we were still in each other's lives...even if we weren't living together.

Chapter 6

Our wedding was breathtakingly beautiful!

It was as if we were transported back in time where ancient oak trees canopied our intimate outdoor ceremony. Or, maybe it was because our guests were *literally* transported, by van, to our outdoor paradise.

Either way, it felt magical.

And, because of my equine love, David had arranged for my father and me to arrive by horse and carriage. I felt like a princess as our horse pranced along the winding road, chauffeuring my father and me into the presence of our guests.

The first person I saw was David. As I looked at him, I felt so loved. So wanted.

My nephew, as well as other close friends, stood alongside David.

My dear bridesmaids, including the high school friend who introduced me to David, greeted me with delight.

In the front row, David's father sat stoically

beside a chair that bolstered a picture of a beautiful woman. A woman I never got to meet. A deeply loved woman who touched the hearts and lives of her three sons and her beloved husband.

On my side sat my mother. This was significant because she would come and go throughout my life. So, to have her consistently around for this special occasion, and even help me with my wedding dress, made it all the more celebratory and treasured.

All these faces greeted me. My stepmother. My sister and brother. Nieces and nephews. My soon-to-be in-laws. My Jennifer. This wedding was bringing us all together.

Then, just before I began my walk down the aisle, the sweetest of sounds rang out as my bell ringers announced my coming with delicate chimes. Maddison, at three years old, was one of those bell ringers!

I had never seen or attended a traditional wedding before. It seemed like nothing about my family was "traditional." This wedding, this marriage, this *experience*…it was everything I never knew I wanted.

Our vows were exchanged. Our lives were forever changed.

Chapter 7

The first time I've ever boarded a plane was for my honeymoon. I was 28 years old. And, *yes,* I was terrified!

However, I was headed to Kauai...surely I could keep it together for the Garden Island! When we arrived, I was certainly glad I did.

If seven days of paradise weren't enough, I also found out I passed my clinical boards. I was a licensed dental hygienist! So many windows of opportunity were happening for me and I was looking forward to my future more than ever.

Yet, while I was flourishing, my sister, Jennifer, was floundering. Just a few months back from our honeymoon we received another call from her. This time she was going to prison.

David left around 10 p.m. to get Maddison that night. He refused to let me go with him because he knew the area wasn't safe. My nephew wasn't at the home where they had been living. Neither was Maddison. Finally, around midnight, David found Maddison. She was still awake, unbathed, and had not eaten dinner. The women who were supposed to be watching her were high on drugs and let David take Maddison without question. David searched for an open fast food restaurant just so he could feed her.

Around 1 a.m., Maddison came running into my bedroom laughing, "Boo!" as she flung open my bedroom door. I will never forget the smile on her face. Her little feet and hands were filthy and her hair was a tangled mess, but we were laughing at her attempt to "surprise" me and we were just so happy to see each other.

I drew her a bubble bath and afterward the three of us fell asleep while watching a Disney movie. Despite the adrenaline David had been under and the environment Maddison had just come from, there was this "peace which surpasses all understanding" in our home.

***

David and I knew we had to stop this cycle. We filed our third guardianship for Maddison. We could not bear to watch this sweet baby girl end up living a life like my sister and me. David and I refused to watch history repeat itself.

We also had *no idea* how intense this journey would be! We found a different family law attorney who believed in our case. She was a wonderful woman who cared about Maddison's future and knew she could use the law to help our family!

But, again, it *is* next to impossible to terminate a birth mother's rights in California. So, we began the scrutiny of social worker visits and countless counseling sessions to prove we were "safe" and fit to be parents for Maddison.

David and I weren't the only ones to receive counseling; even Maddison underwent counseling sessions. Our home had to remain open, at any time, for social worker visitations. Truthfully, we didn't mind. That was the easy part. The hard part was having to tell my sister I was now attempting to terminate her parental rights over Maddison. My sister. My childhood adoration.

Jennifer, though, had continued down a dark road for so long it was as if I didn't even recognize her. As much as I loved her, I knew in my soul I couldn't let Maddison experience what had happened to us as children. Especially when David and I had so much love for Maddison. We had to fight for her.

The court hearings were intensely intimidating. To be on the stand, all eyes on you. One side for you (my husband and our attorney) and one side against you (my sister and her attorneys).

It broke my heart to be fighting like this with my sister. To be honest, I hated even hearing my attorney explain why my sister was unfit to parent Maddison. She was my sister and I still wanted to protect her.

However, at that point in time, I knew she was so lost and Maddison would suffer. Maddison was so perfectly innocent and full of life. There was no way I could willingly let her be exposed to a lifestyle that would steal all the joy from her precious heart.

So, I fought.

I fought against my sister. I fought against the attacks from her attorneys. I fought against the negative thoughts in my mind. I fought against the panic attacks that Maddison would be taken from me. I fought against the tears that literally seemed to steal the breath from my lungs as I cried in my closet, hiding from Maddison so she wouldn't witness the torment of this battle.

For four years I fought. Yes, *FOUR* years! There were countless days spent with the companionship of anxiety and fear.

But, there were also countless memories of laughter, love, and joy as I treasured each and every moment with Maddison and David. I never knew if the next court date would be the harbinger of change, so I couldn't risk taking any time for granted.

On December 12, 2007 the fight was over. The Superior Court of California ruled in favor of our family. We even received confirmation from the appellate court. It was ironclad. Against all odds, our adoption was finalized. We were officially a family—David, Maddison, and me.

So, we celebrated!

At the adoption finalization, the bailiff (who had witnessed most of the trial) asked if we had special plans afterward.

Special plans? "Yes!" we replied. "We're going to Disneyland!"

And we did. We went to the "happiest place on

earth." Still, it could not hold a candle to the "happy" we had in our hearts.

We officially became a family that day. We had won the battle, but in every battle there are casualties. And, sadly, the relationship with my sister was dead.

Chapter 8

Now that we were a secure family and the court hearings and financial stress had ceased, we knew we wanted to grow our family.

Sure, Maddison was seven years old now, but we would joke that she would make a great big sister…and, before we knew it, a built-in babysitter! All teasing aside, Maddison seemed to genuinely want a little brother or sister. We were happy to see our family grow, but after months of negative pregnancy tests I got concerned.

My doctor reassured me that it was just my body needing time to recover from the years of stress over the adoption. However, months turned into years. And years turned into tears.

I tried everything. Every diet, every exercise, every meditation. Nothing seemed to work. Every medical doctor, every acupuncturist, every naturopath, all told me this: "Don't stress. You're healthy; it'll happen."

In May of 2010, after three years of trying, it did happen! I found out I was pregnant! Any mom who has been trying for years to conceive will understand the joy of learning you're carrying a baby. A precious little life! I beamed with excitement and couldn't wait to tell David he was going to be a daddy again and Maddison, at 10 years old, was finally going to be a big sister! Finewood family of four, here we come!

But, at six weeks, I miscarried. More tears. More discouragement. However, it was this discouragement that changed the course of my life.

During the adoption process, I had pleaded with God to let us be Maddison's parents. The miracle of her adoption proved God's hand was on the entire process.

Yet, somewhere along my spiritual journey I got lost. That picture of Jesus in my bedroom as a little girl seemed far away. The 15-year-old girl in me, who gave her heart to Jesus, wasn't speaking up. I didn't even know where she was.

Instead, I thought there were "many paths" that led to God. I didn't believe that Jesus was the *only* way to God. At that time, I thought it was rather pompous to think that Jesus was the only way to God.

But the miscarriage humbled me. I realized I could not just manifest whatever I wanted from the "universe." So in May of 2010, after miscarrying, I cried out with *all* my heart, "God, what is the truth?"

Within days, I remember pulling into a gas station and finding a sticky note on the fuel pump with handwritten words that read, "For God so loved the world that He gave His only begotten Son—John 3:16". *Hmmm, isn't that a Bible scripture,* I thought. *Weird.*

Then that same week, while shopping at a local store, I walked in front of a man. I politely said, "Pardon me," as I crossed in front of him. He reached out his hand to give me something. I don't know why I accepted, but I reached out my hand and took what he gave me. I left the aisle before I looked at the item in my hand. It was a coin that read, "For God so loved the world that He gave His only begotten Son—John 3:16."

Suddenly, I knew. I *knew!* I knew God was reaching out to me and showing me the truth. I knew He wanted to reconcile me to Himself. To show me the relationship He longed to have with me.

I started slowly at first. Telling no one. All my

friends would think I was crazy for drinking the Christian Kool-Aid!

While alone, I began watching Christian TV sermons, all the while staying in stealth mode. Even hiding it from David.

David, when growing up, had experienced a lot of hypocrisy in the church and was in no way wanting to become "religious." So how could I, his wife, now turn on him and want to learn more about Jesus and the Bible? That's not what he signed up for when he married me.

I couldn't get enough of Joyce Meyer and Joel Osteen. Joyce Meyer became a mother figure to me and encouraged me to study the Bible. To *intimately* know Jesus. To be led by the Holy Spirit. Given her background I related to her past and if God could heal her heart from her wounds, *surely* He could heal mine which paled in comparison.

Then there was Joel Osteen. Always encouraging. Always reminding me of what a great, loving, and powerful Father we have. In fact, it was Joel who led me to pray and ask God to forgive me of my sins. I recommitted myself to make Jesus my Lord and Savior in that same prayer. Joel also inspired me to get into a good Bible-based church and keep God first place in my life. So, I was on a mission to do just that!

I found David's old family Bible, blew the dust off it, and began studying. Who was this Jesus? Why did He show up in my childhood, and again when I was 15? And, how did He have the power to answer my cry after my miscarriage?

I couldn't get *enough* of the Bible. I felt like I was reading a love letter written just to me, explaining *everything!* Why I was created. My purpose. My "family" inheritance. The history of mankind. The history of our planet...even our galaxy!

My nerdy science brain loved learning that "He stretches out the north over empty space; He hangs the earth on nothing" (Job 26:7). Keep in mind, Job has been described as the oldest book in the Bible. How then did he know the earth was round and "floating" in space? That hadn't been scientifically "proven" yet!

Then there is Bible prophecy proving the reliability of scripture. My mind was blown away at the accuracy (you can picture the "mind-blowing" emoji, if that helps!). In all seriousness though, fulfilled prophecy, to me, is just another way of God reaching out to us...that we can trust Him.

Yet most touching to me is the message of love, compassion, mercy, and forgiveness. I was hooked. I wanted *all* God wanted for me.

My next step was to get into a good Bible-based church. How was I going to do that? How was I going to convince David?

I remember telling David that I wanted to go to church. He warned me that if I became one of those crazy Christians, we'd have a problem (I'm laughing as I write this. God certainly has a sense of humor!).

But I understood David's trepidation. So, I prayed that God would lead my family to His church.

I absolutely love when God shows His limitless power in my life. Truly, I brim with adoration when I see Him do things that only He can do!

One day, while driving to the post office and following a detour sign (due to road construction), I giggled when I saw a sign for Wildwood Calvary Chapel church. We'd gone to a couple of churches, but none felt like "home" for us. Wildwood was meeting on Sundays at a local junior high school. I convinced David. So, the three of us attended.

That day, we found our church "home."

Chapter 9

So there I was attending church each week with my family and I was absolutely in *love* with my Bible. Maddison was even enrolled at a private Christian junior high school. So, why then wasn't I getting my positive pregnancy test? I was doing everything right, after all.

I still had so much to learn.

I started focusing on the kingdom of God...on righteousness, peace, and joy. But what did that look like? Fortunately, the Bible has a lot to say about it!

I continued to develop my faith and trust in Jesus. I genuinely pictured Him, in heaven, *real as ever*, helping me. I focused more on Him. I found myself changing each day.

Then, with great excitement, I found myself pregnant again! I bought the baby books, I bought a baby outfit, and I celebrated God for His goodness!

However, when I started spotting I grew concerned. The nurse advised me this can be normal and they scheduled me an appointment to ensure things were fine.

The morning of my appointment I knew something was wrong. David and I were driving to the doctor's office when I lost my baby.

I remember wanting to hide myself from the other mothers as I was pushed through the waiting room in a wheelchair to see my doctor. I wanted to hide because if they saw my face I thought I would incite fear in them. I prayed God would protect their babies.

Even though I knew what had happened, I secretly hoped my doctor would examine me and tell me my baby was still alive. She didn't. Instead, she scheduled me for surgery.

***

My third pregnancy was going to be *the one!* I just knew it! This baby was going to be tough! I would not lose another baby!

Yet, at 14 weeks, I did.

In an effort to avoid having another D&C surgery, my doctor agreed to "treat" me in her office, but during the exam, I began to bleed. Badly. Nurses were called in to help the doctor control the bleeding. Once I was stabilized, my doctor looked me in the eyes and told me I really needed to stop trying to have a baby. My body wasn't capable.

Wasn't capable?

My thoughts tailspinned toward darkness. Every negative word spoken over me: "I'd rather have another dog than a child like her," "She's a worthless child," came flooding back. Then, I personally chimed in: *My mother didn't even want me. I'm incapable of doing any good in this world. My body is broken—I'm not worthy to be called a woman.* A barrage of negativity overwhelmed my brain.

I allowed those thoughts to invalidate me from ever carrying babies...right there in that doctor's office.

I even remember thinking: *If this is how God is, I don't want anything to do with Him.*

But it was during my recovery that I experienced a comfort like I'd never before. I was experiencing a *supernatural* comfort. I felt as if I was being lifted up out of my current pain and into a place of *peace*. It sounds strange even trying to explain it now, but I experienced, in real life, God's Word come to life: "Blessed are those who mourn, for they shall be comforted" (Matthew 5:4).

That was enough for me. I knew God was with me. I didn't understand why I kept having miscarriages, but I knew God was with me. He would walk me through this. Jesus met me in the valley of the shadow of death and walked me through it.

Chapter 10

While I was struggling with health issues, someone else was flourishing. My sister.

For obvious reasons, our paths parted ways after the adoption was finalized. Our hearts were hardened and we didn't want to be in each other's lives.

So, when I received a heartfelt letter written to David and me from her boss, explaining how she had changed her course in life and was thriving I, well, didn't believe it.

I wanted to believe it, but I didn't. I didn't want her to come in and upset our family again.

However, when Jennifer reached out to me and I heard her voice...I *missed* her. I wanted her back in my life. But, I was terrified.

We started slowly at first. A dinner every now and then when she was in California. Then she flew me out to Pennsylvania where she was living. We walked through the awkwardness of getting to know each other again. To trust each other again.

She confessed it was the adoption that finally awakened her from the oppressive dark life she'd been living and moved her into the freedom of her current life.

She was also staying sober and using her "*experienced*" criminal mindset to actually help people. Although she was a convicted felon, this company had taken a chance by hiring her. She now oversees the entire security surveillance division. She literally protects those she would have once robbed.

While I was beyond proud and happy for my sister, I had my own demons to conquer. I was desperately afraid that if I let Jennifer back into my life, Maddison might choose her over me. That I would no longer be "worthy" to be her mother. That Jennifer would be better in Maddison's eyes and she would want her to be her mother. This would be another "loss" I couldn't bear. So I didn't tell Maddison that I had rekindled a relationship with Jennifer. At least not in the beginning.

As the months turned into years, Jennifer continued to show her dedication to our family. She and I grew more and more close, and I knew I wanted to share Jennifer with Maddison. But how?

It was a delicate situation. How do we reunite? Would it destroy the family that David, Maddison, and I had so painstakingly, yet lovingly, created?

Then God showed me. He made it crystal clear. My body couldn't carry babies, but Jennifer's could. Our family wasn't destroyed. Our family was just getting started.

My sister, my beautiful sister, gave me the most precious gift...the gift of motherhood! I get to experience being Maddison's mother because of Jennifer.

I *know* God could have healed my body and allowed me to carry babies. I genuinely believe that. But how, then, would I ever have seen the beauty in our story? How would I have witnessed, for myself, the truth found in Isaiah 61:3?

"To console those who mourn in Zion,

To give them beauty for ashes,

The oil of joy for mourning,

The garment of praise for the spirit of heaviness;

That they may be called trees of righteousness,

The planting of the Lord, that He may be glorified."

God redeemed my painful past and turned it into glory. His glory. It's evidence that His grace can heal the unhealable. His power can break unbreakable bonds that hold us captive. His holiness can inspire us to turn from unholy ways. His *love* can soften the hardest of hearts and enable us to love again.

What Satan meant for harm, God used for good and restored my family!

***

Maddison is now 21 years old. It's taken that long to share our story. So, why tell it now? Why share all the dark details? Why share all the pain? The poor choices? Why? Because I know there are countless others who are stuck in their darkness. Who can barely breathe because of the pain. Who feel lost or hopeless. Who are enraged with bitterness and anger for the wrongs done to them. Who are crippled with guilt for the wrongs they've done to others. Or, who carry so much shame they don't think themselves worthy of having beauty in their lives. Some may even feel unworthy of living. They don't see themselves as Jesus does.

I am praying my story helps to stop these sabotaging mindsets and, instead, brings hope and healing to those unable to move forward. My family story may have had abominable beginnings, and I made a myriad of wrong choices along the way, but my family's ending is triumphant! We have experienced *God!* We know what it feels like to overflow with love, joy, and peace!

I marvel that I could be missing out on this wonderful new relationship with my sister had I rejected her request to come back into my life. And, my parents! My amazing parents! I know they did the best they knew how with the examples they'd been given. They, too, suffered much in childhood, but my love and compassion has grown even deeper for them!

I long for anyone who does not yet know Jesus the way I do to open their hearts and minds to the greatest Love they will ever experience.

I still have friends and family members who don't

want to know God. And, the world is filled with others who refuse Jesus. This crushes me. No, really, my heart literally hurts over this, but I sincerely understand their apprehension...because I was once there, too.

However, I have tasted and seen that the Lord is good. I have experienced the peace that surpasses understanding. I have watched God's promises come to life.

I desperately long for my friends and family, *anyone reading this,* to experience this same kind of intimacy with God. To be in awe of Him. To know that Jesus is real. He died for us. He conquered sin and death in this world. He longs to have a relationship with us. And, that He can be trusted...He *should* be trusted. Jesus liberates us from the chains we were never created to carry. My heart is moved with mercy for those who refuse Him because I now *know* His ways are so much better.

So, I will share my story. I will choose Love. Love over negative thoughts. Love over fear. Love over pain, anxiety, and unforgiveness. Love over unbelief. Because Love will never fail. With all my heart, I invite you: Come and see for yourself the consequences of Love.

"Love suffers long and is kind; love does not envy; love does not parade itself, is not puffed up; does not behave rudely, does not seek its own, is not provoked, thinks no evil; does not rejoice in iniquity, but rejoices in the truth; bears all things, believes all things, hopes all things, endures all things. Love never fails."

~ 1 Corinthians 13:4-8

Scriptural Medicine Cabinet

The following scriptures were some of my favorites to help me "retrain my brain." To help me understand the *truth* from lies. I jokingly refer to it as my "medicine." But, one caveat, just like any medicine you have to actually *take it* for it to work. So, meditate on these scriptures. Say them out loud. Let them sink deep into your heart...become a part of you. You can't overdose! In fact, "take" these words when you don't need them and they'll be there for you when you do!

I've provided an opportunity for you to reflect and write down for yourself any personal "ailments" that you've been battling. I've then included a section for you to personalize your "prescription" with scriptures that you've found healing. This can also serve as a resource for you, should you need repeating.

FEAR

I've heard it said that "Fear Not" is the most repeated command in the Bible. And, that makes sense. It seems, daily, I encounter someone grappling with fear. Fear for their health. Fear they might lose their job. Fear for their children. Fear, fear, fear. It's a four-letter word that we must abolish from our mindsets!

"Be strong and of good courage, do not fear nor be afraid of them; for the Lord your God, He is the One who goes with you. He will not leave you nor forsake you."

~ Deuteronomy 31:6

"Have I not commanded you? Be strong and of good courage; do not be afraid, nor be dismayed, for the Lord your God is with you wherever you go."

~ Joshua 1:9

"[Jesus] said to the ruler of the synagogue, 'Do not be afraid; only believe.'"

~ Mark 5:36

"For God has not given us a spirit of fear, but of power and of love and of a sound mind."

~ 2 Timothy 1:7

"There is no fear in love; but perfect love casts out fear, because fear involves torment. But he who fears has not been made perfect in love."

~ 1 John 4:18

My current "ailment":

_____
_____
_____
_____
_____
_____
_____
_____
_____

My personal scriptural Rx:

_____
_____
_____
_____
_____
_____
_____
_____
_____

MURMURING

I had a friend whose son was diagnosed with a heart murmur. It turned out not to be serious. Yet, there is a type of murmur that can be very serious. It's the murmur we mutter from our mouth. Complaining, always finding fault, or just having a pessimistic attitude won't serve us. In fact, it'll keep us grounded in bitterness or enable us to indulge in a "I'm a victim" mindset. I had to get honest with myself and ask, "Do I really want what I've been saying or thinking?" Fortunately, God's Word is here to rescue us from this dangerous entrapment.

"Whoever guards his mouth and tongue keeps his soul from troubles."

~ Proverbs 21:23

"The words of a wise man's mouth are gracious, but the lips of a fool shall swallow him up."

~ Ecclesiastes 10:12

*"Let no corrupt word proceed out of your mouth,
but what is good for necessary edification, that it
may impart grace to the hearers."*

~ Ephesians 4:29

*"Do all things without complaining and
disputing."*

~ Philippians 2:14

*"Rejoice always, pray without ceasing, in
everything give thanks; for this is the will of God
in Christ Jesus for you."*

~ 1 Thessalonians 5:16-18

My current "ailment":

_____

_____

_____

_____

_____

_____

_____

_____

_____

My personal scriptural Rx:

_____

_____

_____

_____

_____

_____

_____

_____

_____

OVERWHELMED

This emotion used to plague me daily! My morning commute would overwhelm me. My workload. My family. The laundry. Yes, I said it, the laundry! Here I had overcome so many obstacles in my life, yet I was letting this *feeling* bully me. But feelings aren't facts. I began searching God's Word for the truth. I discovered God *never* created us to live in this oppressed state. His compassion is wondrous and He has *a lot* to say about bringing our cares, whether great or small, to Him.

"You will keep him in perfect peace, whose mind is stayed on You, because he trusts in You."

~ Isaiah 26:3

"But when He saw the multitudes, He was moved with compassion for them, because they were weary and scattered, like sheep having no shepherd."

~ Matthew 9:36

"Come to Me, all you who labor and are heavy laden, and I will give you rest. Take My yoke upon you and learn from Me, for I am gentle and lowly in heart, and you will find rest for your souls. For My yoke is easy and My burden is light."

~ Matthew 11:28-30

"And He said to me, 'My grace is sufficient for you, for My strength is made perfect in weakness.' Therefore most gladly I will rather boast in my infirmities, that the power of Christ may rest upon me."

~ 2 Corinthians 12:9

"Casting all your care upon Him, for He cares for you."

~ 1 Peter 5:7

My current "ailment":

_____
_____
_____
_____
_____
_____
_____
_____

My personal scriptural Rx:

_____
_____
_____
_____
_____
_____
_____
_____

ANGER

Irritability, resentment, anger...ever felt one of these emotions? Or, have you been easily offended by someone or something? I have certainly been bitten by these emotions and felt the fallout that ensues. There's no question I've witnessed anger's ravenous hunger seize too many lives. Not all anger leads to sin, but when it consumes you it opens the door for the enemy. Fortunately, God's Word is mighty, full of power, and able to turn your anger into peace if you'll abide in Him. He even promises us a blessing! I want God's blessing in my life, so I meditate on these scriptures as my anger antidote.

"For You, Lord, are good, and ready to forgive, and abundant in mercy to all those who call upon You."

~ Psalm 86:5

"Do not say, 'I will recompense evil'; wait for the Lord, and He will save you."

~Proverbs 20:22

"Do not be overcome by evil, but overcome evil with good."

~ Romans 12:21

"So then, my beloved brethren, let every man be swift to hear, slow to speak, slow to wrath."

~ James 1:19

"Not returning evil for evil or reviling for reviling, but on the contrary blessing, knowing that you were called to this, that you may inherit a blessing."

~ 1 Peter 3:9

My current "ailment":

_____

_____

_____

_____

_____

_____

_____

_____

_____

My personal scriptural Rx:

_____

_____

_____

_____

_____

_____

_____

_____

_____

ANXIETY

I used to suffer from thoughts that something bad was going to happen. From earthquakes to fires, my mind would torment me with imminent danger. That was before I knew the love of Jesus. His Word reveals His heart for how we should think, speak, and act. Do I still have these thoughts? Yes. Do I know how to fight them? *Absolutely!* I no longer allow my brain to ruminate on uncertain outcomes because *I know* God promises to protect me and to always be with me. I now understand that my anxiousness is simply my body warning me that I've been thinking incorrectly. My remedy is God's Word, which douses the wildfire caused by anxiety.

"Cast your burden on the Lord, and He shall sustain you; He shall never permit the righteous to be moved."

~ Psalm 55:22

"In the multitude of my anxieties within me, Your comforts delight my soul."

~ Psalm 94:19

"Blessed is the man who trusts in the Lord, and whose hope is the Lord."

~ Jeremiah 17:7

"Casting down arguments and every high thing that exalts itself against the knowledge of God, bringing every thought into captivity to the obedience of Christ."

~ 2 Corinthians 10:5

"Be anxious for nothing, but in everything by prayer and supplication, with thanksgiving, let your requests be made known to God; and the peace of God, which surpasses all understanding, will guard your hearts and minds through Christ Jesus."

~ Philippians 4:6-7

My current "ailment":

_____

_____

_____

_____

_____

_____

_____

_____

_____

My personal scriptural Rx:

_____

_____

_____

_____

_____

_____

_____

_____

_____

JEALOUSY

Jealousy can present its ugly self in many forms: covetousness, distrust, defensiveness, and even comparison. I believe it's rooted in insecurity. The antidote? Receive your security from God. He made you. He knows your strengths and weaknesses, and He adores you! You are His masterpiece so don't compare yourself to others. Instead, walk with the Holy Spirit and embrace being the unique *you* that He created. And learn to appreciate others for their uniqueness, too!

"I say then: Walk in the Spirit, and you shall not fulfill the lust of the flesh."

~ Galatians 5:16

"But the fruit of the Spirit is love, joy, peace, longsuffering, kindness, goodness, faithfulness, gentleness, self-control."

~ Galatians 5:22-23

"For we are His workmanship, created in Christ Jesus for good works, which God prepared beforehand that we should walk in them."

~ Ephesians 2:10

"Finally, brethren, whatever things are true, whatever things are noble, whatever things are just, whatever things are pure, whatever things are lovely, whatever things are of good report, if there is any virtue and if there is anything praiseworthy—meditate on these things."

~ Philippians 4:8

"But you are a chosen generation, a royal priesthood, a holy nation, His own special people, that you may proclaim the praises of Him who called you out of darkness into His marvelous light."

~ 1 Peter 2:9

My current "ailment":

_____

_____

_____

_____

_____

_____

_____

_____

_____

My personal scriptural Rx:

_____

_____

_____

_____

_____

_____

_____

_____

_____

SECURITY

Can we really trust God? Is He really a good God? When I first became a believer I genuinely wanted to know. If God is good, then why did so many bad things happen? I'd hear Christians speak about God's goodness, that He *is* trustworthy, and we *are* secure in Him. But, for me, I needed to personally experience this security and goodness. How did this happen? I spent time with Him. Each morning, and all throughout the day, I'd talk to Him. I would ask Him questions. I'd spend time reading my Bible. I made *time* for Him. And He *always* responded. Today, it is still the same. I challenge you to seek Him. To bring to Him those tough questions. Spend time in His Word...the answers are there.

"For God so loved the world that He gave His only begotten Son, that whoever believes in Him should not perish but have everlasting life."

~ John 3:16

"But none of these things move me; nor do I count my life dear to myself, so that I may finish my race

with joy, and the ministry which I received from the Lord Jesus, to testify to the gospel of the grace of God."

~ Acts 20:24

"And do not be conformed to this world, but be transformed by the renewing of your mind, that you may prove what is that good and acceptable and perfect will of God."

~ Romans 12:2

"Now then, we are ambassadors for Christ, as though God were pleading through us: we implore you on Christ's behalf, be reconciled to God. For He made Him who knew no sin to be sin for us, that we might become the righteousness of God in Him."

~ 2 Corinthians 5:20-21

My current "ailment":

_____

_____

_____

_____

_____

_____

_____

_____

My personal scriptural Rx:

_____

_____

_____

_____

_____

_____

_____

_____

A Prayer to Invite God into Your Heart

"...repentance toward God and faith toward our Lord Jesus Christ."

~ Acts 20:21

If you don't know God, then I invite you to open your heart and pray this prayer:

"God, I want to know You. You came into this world, died for me, and rose again conquering death. In You, Jesus, I have eternal life. Thank You for loving me and forgiving me of my sins. I put my faith and trust in You, Jesus, and make You my Lord and Savior."

Now, fall in love with your Bible. It is your love letter. Your glorious inheritance! And know that with Jesus, there is more to come.

This isn't "The End."

Acknowledgments

I would have never even considered writing this book had it not been for my heavenly Father who walked me through the valley and set me high upon a rock. I am genuinely overjoyed in the love I've found in Him.

For my amazing husband who has stood by my side through thick and thin, and continues to bless me daily with his love, protection, and strength.

For my daughter, Maddison, or as I lovingly call you, my "Boo." I will live the rest of my life expressing the joy of being your mother! You are going to do great things in this life for Jesus!

For my sister, Jennifer. My, oh my, the life we have lived! There is no one I'd rather share my life with than you.

For my mom, dad, and stepmom. We may not have had the "ideal" family, but we *are* family and I love and respect you for all you did for me!

For my nephew, Richie, I will always treasure the years you lived with David and me. You and your family are more special to me than you'll ever know!

For my father-in-law and brothers, thank you for your love, support, and welcoming me into your family...and for raising the best man in the whole wide world!

For my ever-growing extended family, whether near or far, may we learn to grow together and celebrate each other as we enjoy the meaning of *family*.

About the Author

Dianna Finewood has felt a strong calling to serve others through her powerful testimony and inspire them to reach out to Jesus for healing, truth, strength, and guidance, and to embrace forgiveness and grow spiritually in their walk with the Lord. Her hope is that this glimpse into a portion of her life achieves a greater connection between the reader and our heavenly Father.

She, her husband, and their college-age daughter call Southern California their home. In addition to running their sports equipment company, Dianna enjoys horseback riding, Pilates, nutrition, hiking with her husband and daughter, and time spent with friends and family.

www.ingramcontent.com/pod-product-compliance
Lightning Source LLC
LaVergne TN
LVHW041231080426
835508LV00011B/1157